A DAY

by Robin Nelson

Lerner Publications Company · Minneapolis

A **calendar** keeps track of
days, weeks, and **months.**

S	M	T	W	TH	F	S		S	M	T	W	TH	F	S		S	M	T	W	TH	F	S
January								**February**								**March**						
	1	2	3	4	5								1	2							1	2
6	7	8	9	10	11	12		3	4	5	6	7	8	9		3	4	5	6	7	8	9
13	14	15	16	17	18	19		10	11	12	13	14	15	16		10	11	12	13	14	15	16
20	21	22	23	24	25	26		17	18	19	20	21	22	23		17	18	19	20	21	22	23
27	28	29	30	31				24	25	26	27	28				24/31	25	26	27	28	29	30

S	M	T	W	TH	F	S		S	M	T	W	TH	F	S		S	M	T	W	TH	F	S
April								**May**								**June**						
	1	2	3	4	5	6				1	2	3	4								1
7	8	9	10	11	12	13		5	6	7	8	9	10	11		2	3	4	5	6	7	8
14	15	16	17	18	19	20		12	13	14	15	16	17	18		9	10	11	12	13	14	15
21	22	23	24	25	26	27		19	20	21	22	23	24	25		16	17	18	19	20	21	22
28	29	30						26	27	28	29	30	31			23/30	24	25	26	27	28	29

S	M	T	W	TH	F	S		S	M	T	W	TH	F	S		S	M	T	W	TH	F	S
July								**August**								**September**						
	1	2	3	4	5	6						1	2	3		1	2	3	4	5	6	7
7	8	9	10	11	12	13		4	5	6	7	8	9	10		8	9	10	11	12	13	14
14	15	16	17	18	19	20		11	12	13	14	15	16	17		15	16	17	18	19	20	21
21	22	23	24	25	26	27		18	19	20	21	22	23	24		22	23	24	25	26	27	28
28	29	30	31					25	26	27	28	29	30	31		29	30					

S	M	T	W	TH	F	S		S	M	T	W	TH	F	S		S	M	T	W	TH	F	S
October								**November**								**December**						
	1	2	3	4	5								1	2		1	2	3	4	5	6	7
6	7	8	9	10	11	12		3	4	5	6	7	8	9		8	9	10	11	12	13	14
13	14	15	16	17	18	19		10	11	12	13	14	15	16		15	16	17	18	19	20	21
20	21	22	23	24	25	26		17	18	19	20	21	22	23		22	23	24	25	26	27	28
27	28	29	30	31				24	25	26	27	28	29	30		29	30	31				

There are 365 days in a **year.**

A month has between 28
and 31 days.

There are 24 hours in a day.

A day is everything you do
from one morning to the next.

In the morning, I eat
breakfast.

In school, I read a book.

I write numbers on the board.

I eat lunch with my friends.

I sing songs in music class.

I play basketball.

After school, I play with my
brother.

I eat dinner with my family.

I brush my teeth.

My dad reads me a book
before I go to bed.

What is your day like?

What is your day like?

You can make a pie graph to show what you do in a day. The circle is one day, or 24 hours. Look at the pie graph on the right to find how many hours were spent eating. How many hours do you spend eating? How many hours were spent playing? How many hours do you spend playing?

One Child's Day

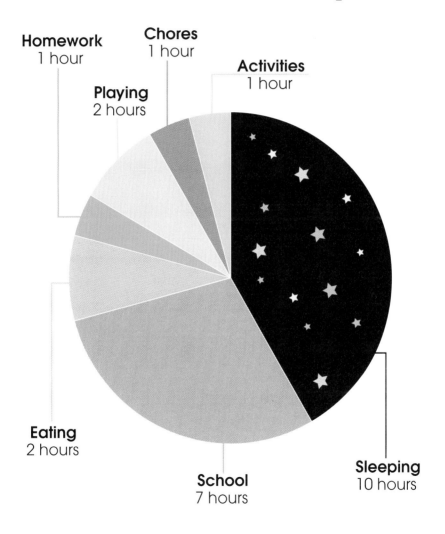

Homework
1 hour

Chores
1 hour

Playing
2 hours

Activities
1 hour

Eating
2 hours

School
7 hours

Sleeping
10 hours

Fun Day Facts

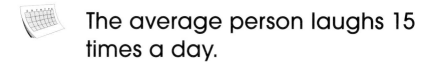 The average person laughs 15 times a day.

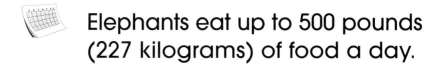 Elephants eat up to 500 pounds (227 kilograms) of food a day.

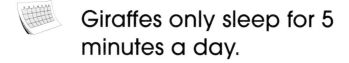 Giraffes only sleep for 5 minutes a day.

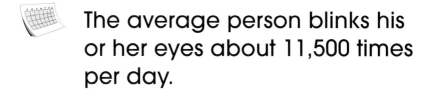 The average person blinks his or her eyes about 11,500 times per day.

The earth turns completely once in a day.

Americans use 5,506,540 gallons (20,844,456 liters) of water each day for showers.

 A hen produces one egg in a day.

 Bamboo (the tallest grass in the world) can grow up to 36 inches (90 centimeters) in a day.

Glossary

 calendar – a report that keeps track of days, weeks, and months

 day – the time from one morning to the next morning. A day is 24 hours.

 month – a part of the year. There are 12 months in a year.

 week – an amount of time. There are 7 days in a week.

 year – an amount of time. There are 12 months in a year.

Index

The photographs in this book are reproduced through the courtesy of: © Todd Strand/Independent Picture Service, front cover, pp. 2, 3, 4, 5, 9, 22 (all); © Art Morris/Visuals Unlimited, p. 6; © Jeff Greenberg/Visuals Unlimited, p. 7; © Jeffry W. Myers/Photo Network, pp. 8, 10; © Trip/S. Grant, pp. 11, 13; © Dennis MacDonald/Photo Network, p. 12; © Myrleen Ferguson Cate/Photo Network, pp. 14, 15; © Vic Bider/Photo Network, p. 16; © Stockbyte, p. 17.

Lerner Publications Company
A division of Lerner Publishing Group
241 First Avenue North
Minneapolis, MN 55401 U.S.A.

Website address: www.lernerbooks.com

Library of Congress Cataloging-in-Publication Data

Nelson, Robin, 1971–
    A day / by Robin Nelson.
        p.   cm. — (First step nonfiction)
    Includes index.
    ISBN: 0–8225–0177–5 (lib. bdg. : alk. paper)
    1. Calendar—Juvenile literature. 2. Days—Juvenile literature.
[1. Days. 2. Calendar.] I. Title. II. Series.
CE85.N43 2002
529'.1—dc21   2001002204

Manufactured in the United States of America
1 2 3 4 5 6 – AM – 07 06 05 04 03 02